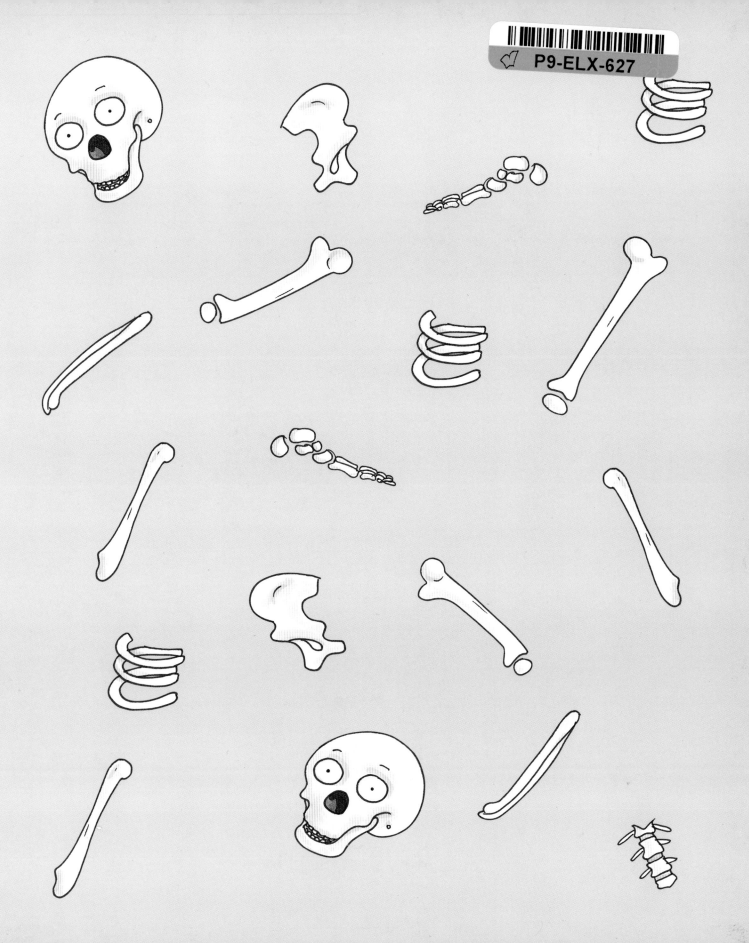

Contents

YOUR AMAZING BODY

BACK PACK BOOKS

· NEW YORK

ON THE OUTSIDE

Look in a mirror. What do you see?
You see the outside of your body—your skin
and your eyes, ears, nose, and mouth.

All these parts have something in common:
they are sensitive. They sense what is around
you, so you know what's happening.

From head to toe

Your skin protects your inside parts from bumps
and knocks, from germs and from drying out.
It also protects you from the sun's powerful
rays. Skin, like all your body parts, is made of
cells. They are so tiny that 10 million of them
would fit inside this letter "o."

Repair work

Skin easily repairs small cuts and
scrapes. If you cut your knee, it bleeds
at first. Next, the blood hardens, and a
scab forms as new skin grows under it. After
a week or two, your knee is as good as new!

Which sense?

Which body parts would you use when watching your favorite singer, Suzy Star?

 Hurry and find the right stickers before the show is over!

You eat your favorite popcorn.

You're so excited you have goosebumps all over!

Five senses

You smell the hot and sweaty audience.

You listen as Suzy sings her latest number one song.

You admire Suzy's bright purple clothes.

Mmm, tasty!

You taste with your tongue, but not all of it. The main, upper part of your tongue can't taste anything, but the edges can.

Here are the four taste areas on the tongue.

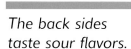 *The back sides taste sour flavors.*

The front sides detect salty tastes.

The back of the tongue detects bitter tastes.

The front tip is best at detecting sweet flavors.

9

Look and listen!

For most people, the most important sense is sight. You're using your eyes to read as you look at these worms—sorry, words! Hearing is your next most important sense. Close your eyes and listen. Even in a quiet place, there are always sounds.

Big eyes

Owls have big eyes to help them hunt for food at night. In the dark the round hole in the middle of the owl's eye, its pupil, gets bigger. It lets in lots of light so the owl can see. Your eyes do the same in the dark. During the day, when it is brighter, your pupils get smaller and let in less light.

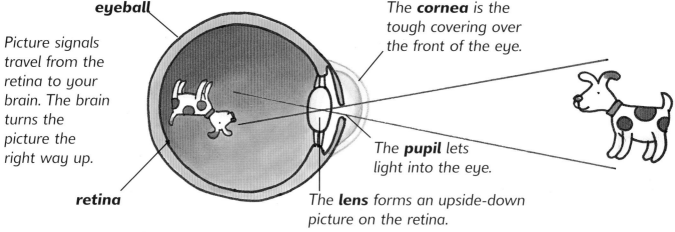

eyeball

Picture signals travel from the retina to your brain. The brain turns the picture the right way up.

retina

*The **cornea** is the tough covering over the front of the eye.*

*The **pupil** lets light into the eye.*

*The **lens** forms an upside-down picture on the retina.*

Fun fact

You blink every few seconds, for about a quarter of a second each time. During one day, your eyes are closed for over 30 minutes altogether. That's blinking amazing!

Ears at work

Boom! Crash! Tinkle! Your ears hear thousands of different sounds. These sounds can be loud or quiet, low or high, harsh or pleasant. When you sleep, your eyes are closed but your ears keep on working. A loud or strange sound will wake you up.

Take a look at the middle and inner parts of the ear. They're inside the head!

Not too loud!

Very loud sounds can damage your ears and harm your hearing. If you wear headphones and the person next to you can hear your music, that means it's too loud!

Body words

balance: being able to stay upright when you stand or move.
pupil: a hole in the middle of the colored part of the eye.
retina: a lining at the back of the eye that detects light.

Look and listen!

Wobble, totter, sway!

Balance stops you from falling over when you stand or move. Some people call it your body's "sixth sense." Your ears help you balance. They tell you which way is up even when you're in the dark.

11

INSIDE YOUR BODY

If you look inside a car engine or a computer, you will see lots of parts. Your body also has lots of parts, but it's much more complicated!

All your body parts work together in special groups, or systems, to keep you alive and well.

Lots of bones

Bones make up one quarter of your body weight. You have 206 different ones, which make up your skeleton. Bones are hard, stiff, and strong. They hold up soft, flexible parts, such as the stomach and nerves.

See the bones inside the legs and feet. You have 31 bones in each leg: five in the hip and leg, seven in the ankle, and 19 in the foot.

Twist and turn

Your back is not one single bone—it's made up of 26 small bones called vertebrae. These bones are joined together in a long row. All the vertebrae work together so you can twist and turn.

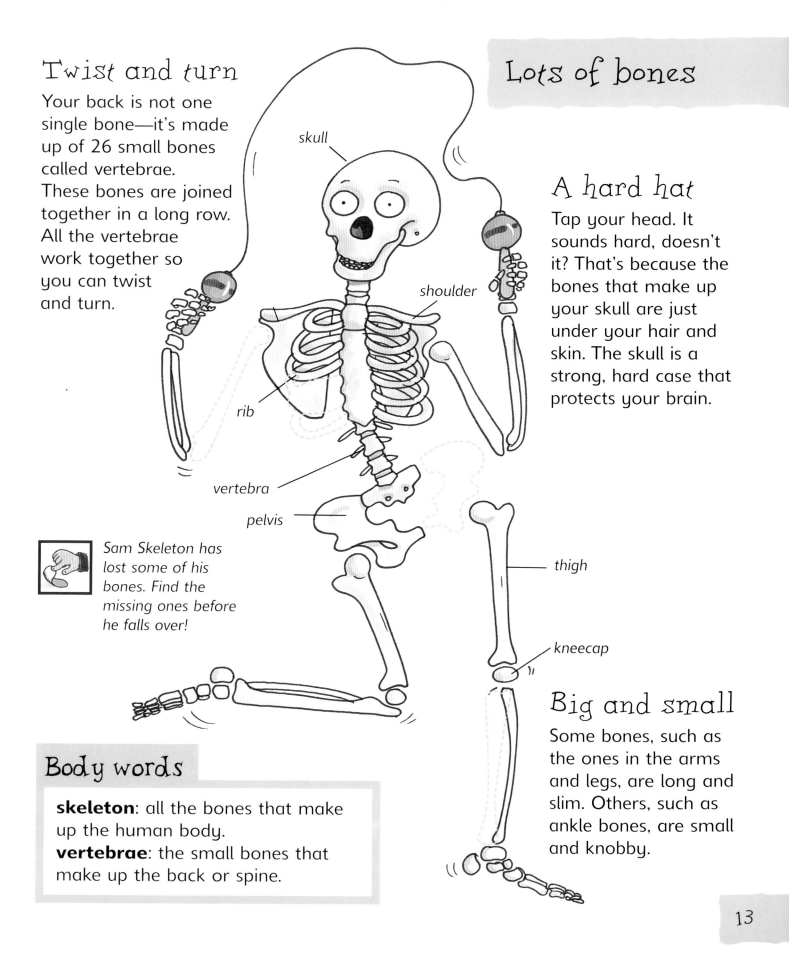

skull

shoulder

rib

vertebra

pelvis

thigh

kneecap

Sam Skeleton has lost some of his bones. Find the missing ones before he falls over!

Lots of bones

A hard hat

Tap your head. It sounds hard, doesn't it? That's because the bones that make up your skull are just under your hair and skin. The skull is a strong, hard case that protects your brain.

Big and small

Some bones, such as the ones in the arms and legs, are long and slim. Others, such as ankle bones, are small and knobby.

Body words

skeleton: all the bones that make up the human body.
vertebrae: the small bones that make up the back or spine.

13

Mostly muscles

Every move you make, from blinking an eye to jumping up high, is powered by your muscles. Almost half of your body is made of muscles. And there are lots of them—over 600! Most are long and slim, and joined at each end to bones.

Pulling power

Muscles make your body twist, turn, push, and pull. But a muscle on its own cannot twist, turn, or push—it can only pull. Each of your bones has lots of muscles all around it. They work in turn to move the bone in different directions.

See below what happens to your muscles when you bend your arm.

pulling with arm muscles

\
muscle

Bent or straight arm?

When you bend your arm, the muscle at the front tightens and grows shorter, pulling your arm up. The muscle at the back relaxes, letting your arm bend.

When your arm is straight, the muscle at the front relaxes and grows longer, while the one at the back shortens.

Back power!

Sometimes you can pull harder by keeping your arms straight and pulling with the strong muscles of your back.

pulling with back muscles

Learning to move

Your brain sends signals to your muscles along nerves. Luckily, the brain can move whole groups of muscles together. It would take a long time to control each of your 600 muscles separately. Writing your name would take all day!

Making faces

Save effort and energy—frown less and smile more! Here's why ...

Hee-hee-hee!

When you smile or grin, you use about 20 muscles in your face. The main one in each cheek pulls the corner of your mouth out and up.

Boo-hoo-hoo!

A frown or scowl uses about 40 muscles, which is twice as many as a smile. One of these muscles is in the side of your chin. It pulls the corner of your mouth out and down.

15

In and out

What do you do every few seconds, every day, for all your life, almost without thinking? You breathe. Your body must breathe to take in fresh air. It needs a gas in the air, called oxygen, to stay alive. In, out, in, out, in ...

How breathing happens

You breathe air in through the nose and mouth, down the throat and windpipe, into the two lungs inside your chest.

In the lungs, oxygen from the air is taken into the blood, which carries it all around your body. The used air comes back up the windpipe and out again.

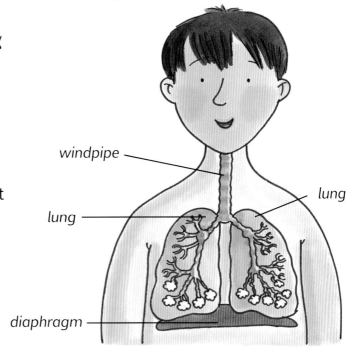

windpipe

lung

lung

diaphragm

Staying alive

Every tiny part, or cell, in your body uses oxygen. It lets your body get the energy out of the food you eat. Your body's cells need this energy to carry out their work and keep you alive.

Fun facts

You probably take about 10 million breaths in one year.
When you sneeze, air rushes out of your nose as fast as a race car, at almost 125 miles per hour.

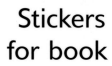
Stickers
for book

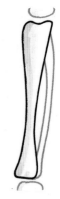

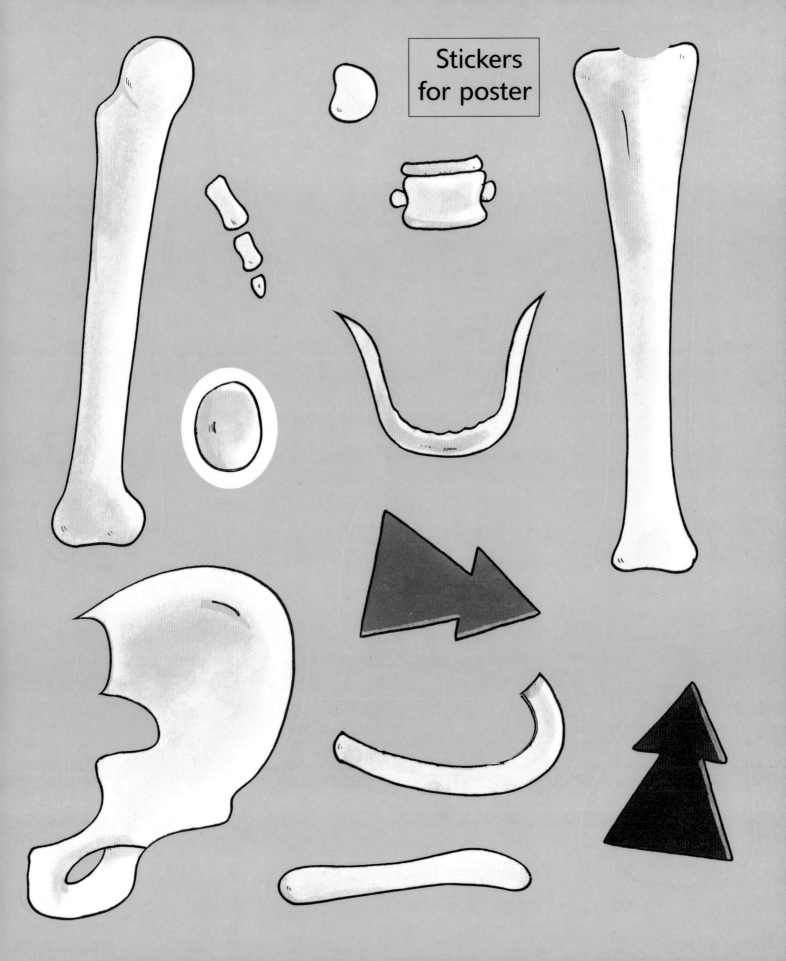

Stickers
for poster

Sucking in

Your breathing muscles stretch and make your lungs bigger to suck in air. The main breathing muscles are the diaphragm, in the bottom of the chest, and the rib muscles.

Blowing out

When you breathe out, the diaphragm and rib muscles relax. The stretched lungs shrink back to their smaller size.

See the differences in the size and shape of the lungs as you take a deep breath and then blow it out.

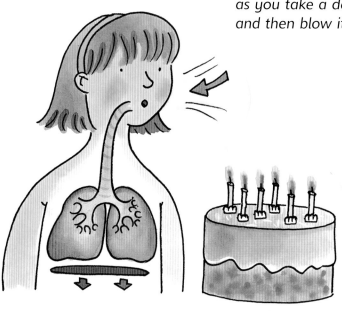

A-tish-ooo!

A sneeze is an extra-fast rush of air that comes up the windpipe and throat and out through your nose. It clears bits of dust and mucus from inside your nose.

Body words

diaphragm: a curved sheet of muscle under the lungs.
lungs: the two body parts on either side of your heart that you use to breathe.
windpipe: a strong, flexible tube that carries air from the nose and throat down to your lungs.

Cough, cough!

A cough is an extra-fast rush of air. It comes up the windpipe and rattles the voice box in your neck. It clears dust and mucus from your throat and breathing tubes.

Round and round

What's red and goes round and round your body? Blood! It flows through tubes called blood vessels and never stops. Your beating heart pumps blood around your body. Blood carries oxygen to all your body parts.

On the move

Blood travels along blood vessels to every corner of your body. Strong, thick-walled tubes called arteries carry fresh blood away from your heart. Flexible, thin-walled tubes called veins bring used blood slowly back to your heart.

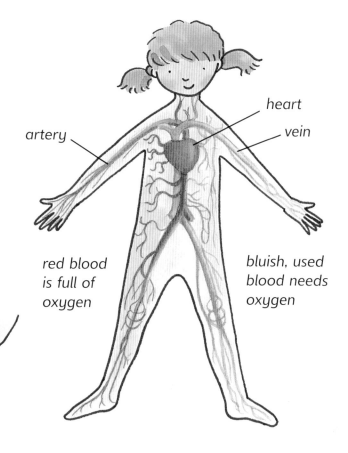

artery

heart

vein

red blood is full of oxygen

bluish, used blood needs oxygen

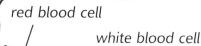

red blood cell

white blood cell

What's in blood?

In a drop of blood as big as this "o," there are over 10 million red cells. They are round and carry oxygen. There are also 20,000 white cells. They are bigger and pale-colored. They keep the blood clean and fight germs.

Carrying information

Nerves look like tiny pieces of shiny, gray string. They carry information from your brain and spinal cord to all the other parts of your body. Some carry information to your muscles, while others carry information about heat, cold, and pain.

Look out!

A reflex is a body action that happens quickly, without your thinking about it. Look at the different dangers below and see how reflexes work.

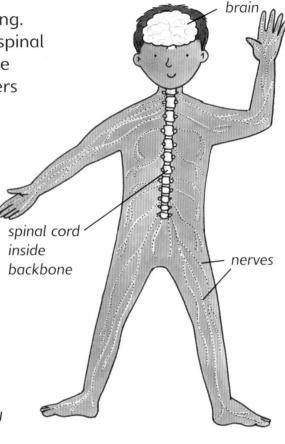

brain

spinal cord inside backbone

nerves

Eyes blink if something comes too close.

Hand pulls away quickly if it feels great heat.

You cough if food goes down your throat the wrong way.

Foot quickly lifts up if it steps on something sharp.

A memory test

How many doors does your home have? Imagine each room in turn, count its doors, and slowly add them up. It's amazing what you can remember when you try!

FROM BABY TO GROWN-UP

Every person begins as a tiny speck. This grows bigger until you are born as a baby. Changes take place in your body during your whole life. You need to look after your body. It has to last you a lifetime!

A new baby

Can you remember your real "birth" day—the day you were born? The answer is "No!" because you were just a tiny baby. Your body did not begin on this day. It grew and developed inside your mother for nine months before.

In the beginning

Pregnancy starts when a tiny egg in the mother joins with an even tinier sperm from the father.

After 1 week
The egg divides itself many times. It forms a cluster of tiny cells.

After 1 month
The baby is the size of this letter "C." It has a face and a beating heart.

After 2 months
The baby is about as big as your thumb. It has eyes, ears, fingers, and toes.

24

After 5 months

The baby is about as big as your fist. It can kick, somersault, and move around in the womb.

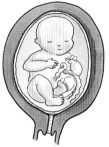

Take a look at the baby inside this pregnant mom. It's almost ready to be born!

Fun fact

A newborn baby can sleep for up to 22 hours a day!

After 9 months

The baby is ready to be born. It floats in a liquid inside the womb. Its surroundings are warm, quiet, and dark. Outside the womb it will be very different!

Being born

After nine months in the womb, the baby is ready to be born. The strong muscles of the mother's womb squeeze hard to push her baby through a passageway into the outside world. Birth is very tiring for the mother and the baby.

Body words

pregnancy: the time, usually about 9 months, when a baby grows inside its mother.
womb: a baby grows inside its mother's womb.

Growing up

When you are 18 years old, your body will be twice as tall as when you were two years old. Even when your body stops getting bigger, parts of you keep on growing—your hair, nails, and skin grow all the time.

From baby to child

As a baby grows and develops, it learns how to do new actions and gains new skills. Every baby is different. So, every baby learns how to do these new things at different times.

About 2 months
Smiles at a friendly face

About 4 months
Grasps a toy put into the hand

About 6 months
Sits up

About 8 months
Crawls around

About 12 months
Takes first steps

How tall are you?

By the time you are two years old, your body has grown half its height. You grow more slowly between the ages of two and ten, and then growth speeds up again until you reach your full height by 20!

9 months   2 years   7 years   18 years

Stay well

There are lots of different ways to keep fit and healthy. Helen feels well because she takes care of herself. She eats healthy foods, exercises, and brushes her teeth twice a day.

Match the right sticker to each of Helen's healthy activities.

Feeling good

Be active!

Walk whenever you get the chance! Participate in sports or exercises that are enjoyable and fun.

Eat properly!

Have regular meals. Eat fresh fruits and vegetables —and not too many fatty foods!

Be healthy!

Visit the doctor for the vaccinations you need. Go to the dentist at least once a year. Have regular eye exams.

Brush your teeth!

Brush your teeth after main meals and before bedtime. Ask your dentist about flossing and using a mouthwash.

Keep clean!

Shower or bath regularly. Comb or brush your hair well.

Stay out of the sun!

Strong sunshine can harm your skin. Protect your skin with sunscreen, and stay in the shade when it's very hot. Stay cool, and wear a sunhat and sunglasses, too!

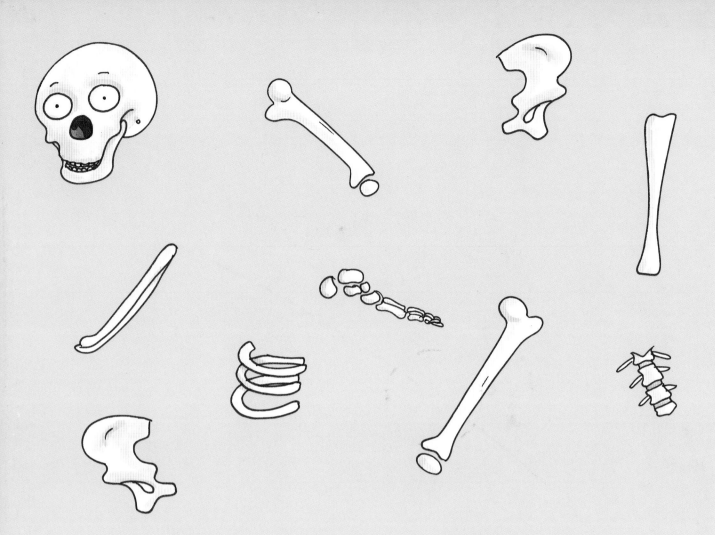

Medical consultant: Dr. Tony Smith, BM Oxon

Copyright © 2003 by Parragon Publishing

This 2005 edition published by Backpack Books,
by arrangement with Parragon Publishing.

Backpack Books
122 Fifth Avenue
New York, NY 10011

ISBN 0-7607-6851-X
Manufactured in China

05 06 07 08 09 MCH 10 9 8 7 6 5 4 3 2 1